A MAXWELL WINSTON STONE SERIES

CHIPPED BUT NOT BROKEN 2

WHEN ADVERSITY ENHANCES THE HUMAN SPIRIT

ERNIE CARWILE

A MAXWELL WINSTON STONE SERIES

CHIPPED BUT NOT BROKEN 2

WHEN ADVERSITY ENHANCES THE HUMAN SPIRIT

ERNIE CARWILE

Verbena Pond Publishing Co., LLC

Second Edition Copyright © 2013 Ernie Carwile Inc.

All rights reserved. Any part of this book may be used or reproduced in any respectable manner whatsoever without the written permission of the publisher as long as the source is cited. For information contact Verbena Pond Publishing Co., L.L.C., P.O. Box 370270, Denver, CO 80237, 303-641-8632

ISBN: 978-0-9796176-7-6

Library of Congress Control Number: 2013 933 6 05

*This book is dedicated to my friend,
Maxwell Winston Stone, whose lessons taught
me the true significance of adversity...
and radically changed my life.*

There Is No Education
Like Adversity.

—Disraeli (1804–1881)
British Prime Minister

When One Door Closes,
Another Opens, But We
Often Look So Long And
So Regretfully Upon The
Closed Door That We
Do Not See The One
Which Is Opened For Us.

—Alexander Graham Bell
(1847–1922)

Prologue

AX WAS SOMETHING to see.

Wherever he went, you'd soon find him surrounded by people, all intently listening, all savoring his words like a rich, hot fudge sundae. You could see it on their faces.

How he garnered such crowds remains a mystery.

Certainly not his stature, for when standing his head usually only reached most people's nose. Nor was it his thin, wiry body, for he was rather scrawny looking, especially with his often three-day, gray-white speckled beard. His demeanor seemed shy, withdrawn.

Yes, his body probably looked like any other old man's body: wizened, used up. But his energetic, fluid movements were more of a young man's, and seemed incongruent with the rest of him.

Then came the eyes: intense, burning brightly, they gave off the kind of electricity seen only in tropical thunderstorms.

I watched him do it over and over, never believing the speed at which the people became corralled, then enthralled, ensconced in his aura. There'd only be a side comment, a murmur of some words, and unaware, they'd be drawn into his spell, then entertained beyond their wildest expectations.

And all through just a story. A tale. Words intricately woven together like a Hopi Indian blanket, symphonic voice inflections, pauses held just the right length, head movements accenting the most important, eyebrows raised and lowered for emphasis, eyes projecting like a movie theater.

Laughing. Frowning. Sighing. Crying. He was the master.

He was the storyteller.

* * * * * *

I want to tell you some things about my friend, Maxwell Winston Stone.

He first came to me in a random *thought*, a kind of dream, where he just magically appeared. Though not *physically visible*, he soon proved to me to be as real anything important in my life, as real as my wife.

Max came to me as I was just beginning to write my first book, ***The Storyteller 1***, and truly took on a life of his own. I talked with him, took counsel from him, and he became my best friend.

Prologue

Take, for example, his name. Do you know how he described the derivation of his full name? Out-of-the-blue, he said that the "Maxwell came from all the coffee his parents drank; Winston, from all the cigarettes they smoked; and as for Stone" ... he paused here and the temperature in the room seemed to drop twenty degrees, "that represented their hearts."

Do you remember the story about Harvey, the invisible rabbit? Max is kind of like that to me, except he didn't follow me around everywhere. He is more like a real friend who lives somewhere else. At first we just *met* intermittently until our friendship ballooned and we began spending a great deal of time together.

Max was able to share his incredible wisdom with me in the form of quotes and short, powerful little anecdotal stories. Never preachy, he was somehow able to know exactly what I needed to hear and his ideas profoundly altered my life.

What you will be reading came directly from my talking to ... and listening to ... Max. I hope you can benefit from his ideas as much as I do.

Introduction

IF YOU ARE LIKE ME, ANYTIME a crisis occurs in my life, a deep-seated belief kicks in which informs me that, first, I have done something wrong to deserve the hair-raising event, and second, that God or the Universe is punishing me for my blunder.

Joining with these beliefs come the corollary beliefs that when things go smoothly in life, I am being rewarded; and the more I behaved well, the more rewards will be granted.

However, I have concluded what most self-reflecting humans discover through life's ordinary maturing process (and especially after reading Rabbi Harold Kushner's book, *When Bad Things Happen to Good People*) that these beliefs have proved to be impregnated with such inconsistencies that a new vision of reality screamed to be discovered. The new insight emerging for me, and certainly one I continue to struggle with because of its disturbing validity, is as follows:

1. The adversities we encounter are a very integral part of everyday life; these seemingly random occurring bumps in the road are as normal as breathing, and happen to all of us whether we have been acting good or badly.
2. Each adversity entering our lives does not represent a form of punishment, but actually contains a hidden gift meant specifically for us and us alone.
3. Furthermore, it is these adversities, and perhaps these alone, that give us character and strength, something we never would have attained without going through the adversities' fire.

Many years ago I facilitated a group of people in a "growth" seminar. After pre-planning a mass of exercises and role-playing situations, for some unplanned reason I impulsively posed to the group the questions: "What were the three best things that happened in your life?" And then, "What were the three worst things?"

Introduction

Without even thinking or considering the question, I blurted out, "Which did you learn the most from?"

The thick silence which followed the spontaneous last question reverberated throughout the room. The reverie was finally broken by someone's exclamation, "Oh, wow!"

In that brief moment we all discovered an amazing, universal truth: *Our adversities teach us much, much more than the sought after good happenings in our lives.* This new idea permeated so thoroughly through our group that one usually very quiet, timid, older lady raised her hand with a most daunting question: "Does this mean the bad things that happen in our lives are actually good things?"

This one isolated instance ignited a fire within me and led me on a journey of extensive reading and of observing people who had achieved success. Over and over again I saw how most people became better human beings only *after* being exposed to great difficulties.

Eventually, despite great internal apprehension and debate, I came to clearly understand that all of us have the opportunity to become better *because of our life's adversities*. I came to see and believe that these adversities make us greater than who we were before their appearance.

My friend, Maxwell Stone, shared with me a wonderful analogy of this new discovery when he compared a person's life with that of the old blacksmith:

> In the process of making a new tool, a blacksmith pumps the billows to raise the temperature of the furnace fire. Then he places a bit of iron until it heats up and achieves a kind of translucent, glass-like state.
>
> Next he removes it from the fire, places it on an anvil, and since it is now in a more pliable state, he is able to pound the iron with a heavy hammer into a new, different shape than it originally held.
>
> Finally, the blacksmith thrusts the hot metal into cold water so that the dramatic temperature change "tempers" the iron, which gives it new strength and durability.

Isn't that just how life is? Our adversities certainly *heat* us up, *beat* us around, and then we are *thrust* into situations that we were not expecting. This is the way the human spirit is formed, developed and strengthened.

Introduction

My hope is that every reader of this book will also experience a shift in their perception of life, and grasp this amazing truth.

Never forget that every person, great or small, in this world of ours has a history of adversity ... Martin Luther King, became great only after being arrested many times simply for leading peace marches and trying to help all races to see their oneness... Helen Keller became great only after overcoming the limitations from being blind and deaf ... Abraham Lincoln's number of election defeats is legendary, and he had to overcome devastating depression to be elected President ... And Franklin Delano Roosevelt's strength in rising above the crippling, emotional and physical effects of polio has been attributed to his later success as President of the United States.

You see, it was as if the adversities which they confronted were foreordained. Max said, "You must be willing to give up who you are now for the person you wish to become." The only requirement, he explained, is for you to allow the change to take place.

This same opportunity is available to everyone. All that is needed is a change—a shift in perception. We simply need to face every adversity with the *foreknowledge* that it holds a precious gift meant just for us. Imagine how differently we would view the world and our individual lives with these new eyes.

The following pages are filled with quotes and stories on this crucially important topic of adversity. Read them. Absorb them. Return to them with every difficulty life lays before you. You too will soon discover one of the greatest secrets of all: By facing every adversity as an opportunity, you will discover a hidden gift meant specifically for you.

Every Person Must Walk Through Their "Fire" Alone. THAT Is What Gives Us Our Strength And Character.

—Maxwell Winston Stone

There Is A Popular Fable Which Says That: The Chinese Have A Written Character For The Word *Crisis*, Which Is Made Up Of Two Equal Symbols. One Stands For DANGER. The Other Stands For OPPORTUNITY.

Do You See The Significance Of This? Too Often We Feel Sorry For Ourselves And Forget That Adversity Holds The Seed Of Opportunity. And We Forget We Are The Ones Who Make The Choice On Which It Will Be.

—**Max**

Adversity Has The Effect of Eliciting Talents Which, In Prosperous Circumstances, Would Have Laid Dormant.

—HORACE ROMAN LYRIC POET
(65BC-8BC)

ONE HEARTWARMING story that came out of the Vietnam War was about a man who had lost an arm and both legs.

He was assigned to 'Nam right after his wife had become pregnant with their first child. Just after his arrival in the foreign jungle, two tragic things happened. First, he stepped on a land mine and lost both legs and an arm; then, he was captured and became a POW for five years. During these horrible years, his wife had given birth to their son, who had grown from a baby to a little boy who had just started kindergarten.

When the POWs were finally released and flown back to the U.S., there were actually two planes involved. One carried the healthier men, who received all of the media attention, while the other plane held the men who had been badly injured. These men were quietly taken off from the backside of the second plane.

Meeting the second plane were the wife and 5-year-old son. The young boy was both nervous and excited because he'd never seen his dad in person before. He watched as his dad was taken off the plane and noticed he didn't have legs. Turning to his mother he whispered, "Mommy, Daddy doesn't have any legs, does he?" His mother, trying to be strong though tears were running down her face replied, "No sweetie, he doesn't."

As the men wheeled his father closer, the little boy saw his dad was missing an arm too. "Mommy," he whispered again, "Daddy doesn't have an arm either, does he?" His mother shook her head no, barely able to keep from bursting into tears.

After a long pause in which one could tell the boy was thinking really hard, he turned to his mom and said a beautiful thing. Leaning over he whispered, "Let's not tell him."

Only When It Is
Dark Enough
Can You See
The Stars.

—Ralph Waldo Emerson (1803-1882)
American Essayist and Poet

DO YOU KNOW WHAT Melba toast is? Do you know anything of its origins?

Melba toast is a dry, crisp thin slice of bread. It is created by lightly toasting both sides of a piece of bread under a grill. Then you slice the browned bread laterally so that it is now one-half its normal size; returning it to the grill, you then toast the untoasted side. The result is a drier and smaller piece of toast with half the calories of a normal piece of bread that is crisp and light.

This toast came about accidently from an adversity–a huge error made by the underling of the famous chef, August Escoffier, at the luxurious Savoy Hotel in London in the year 1897. The Australian opera singer, Dame Nellie Melba, was very ill and limited in what she could eat, living mainly on toast.

One day, while the great chef was preoccupied

with preparing another meal, a young want-to-be chef prepared the great lady's toast. Not paying attention to what his assistant was doing, Escoffier missed that the underling had allowed the toast to bake too long and ended up with a dried-up, parchment-like piece of bread. Escoffier, then noticing the horrible piece of dried bread the famous singer had just bitten into, hurried over to apologize only to hear her exclaim, "How clever of you, Escoffier. I have never eaten such a lovely piece of toast."

Thereafter, it was call "Melba Toast" after the famed opera singer.

It is adversity, the appearance of a mistake or a tragedy, that often brings about the creation of something new and often improved, leaving the characters and our world with something better than before.

The Real Truth
Is That
We're All
Handicapped,
Only Some Of
Our Handicaps
Can't Be Seen
With The
Physical Eyes.

—Maxwell Winston Stone

WHILE OUT WALKING one day a man came upon a ferocious grizzly bear, which began chasing him. The man ran as fast as he could until he had to halt abruptly at the edge of a steep cliff. Seeing no other option, he decided to jump into the canyon below. Fortunately, at the last instant, he noticed a vine at the cliff's edge just long enough to reach the canyon floor below. Quickly scampering over, he cautiously climbed down the vine. After going a ways, he looked down, only to see another ferocious grizzly bear awaiting him at the bottom. While pondering his dire predicament, he noticed above him and slightly out of reach two mice nibbling away on his vine. Frantic, he searched for another escape. To his surprise, he discovered a small strawberry patch growing vertically out of the cliff, one plant heavily laden with the biggest, reddest, most beautiful strawberries he'd ever seen. So he plucked one, ate it, and found it was the best strawberry he'd ever had.

The moral of the story is this: There will always be a bear behind you and a bear in front of you, and usually there will be mice chewing on your lifeline. But in spite of that, if you can still find and enjoy the strawberries in life, you will have truly lived.

SAW ON MY CELL PHONE IT was Max calling.

"What's up, Max?"

"Let's meet for coffee."

"Okay, where?" I asked.

"I found a new little coffeehouse. It's much quieter than Starbucks and Paneras and cozier, too… It's called Dazbog and we can actually hear each other talk there."

"Sounds good," and I repeated, "Where's it located?"

"I guess there're lots of their coffee houses in Denver but the one I stumbled across is at 2450 So. Downing Street," Max said. "I'll meet you there in fifteen minutes."

* * * * * *

I've got to admit, Max knows how to find the best places.

We've had coffee in most every Starbucks Coffee shop and Paneras in Denver and our biggest complaint is that it's often too noisy and just doesn't feel like what we always hoped real coffee houses would feel like.

Walking into the Dazbog, I instantly knew why Max liked it so much. It was charming and emoted warm feelings. The regular tables were there, but we found the comfortable leather couches interspersed made us feel like we wanted to snuggle in and spend the whole day talking and drinking the wonderful coffee. I always get regular black coffee and after one taste I was stunned over its rich flavors.

Of course, Max had already staked out one of the leather couches and I sat across from him.

I am constantly reminded by my wife how different men are from women. When women connect, there's always a lot of hugging and squealing before they even begin to discuss what they've met for; it takes them at least twenty minutes to bring each other up to date on each other's lives.

Men are different. We cut right to the quick. I sat my cup of coffee on the table along with the treat I'd chosen from the array of goodies on the counter, a delicious Snicker Doodle cookie. Max wasted no time; he simply smiled, said hello, and started right off with what he wanted to tell me.

"A new idea popped into my mind, and it's a real doozy."

"Okay," I chuckled, "What is it?"

Max paused, something he always did to increase the drama of what he was going to present, then began. "I'm sure you're aware of the statements people make in regards to cancer. They say such things as, "We are in the fight of our life"… "We're going to beat this thing"… "This is a battle we're going to win."

I waited for a moment before saying, "Sure, you hear it on T.V. or read about it in the newspaper all the time."

"You know how I often get answers to problems in dreams? Well," he continued, "I had one of my most thought-provoking dreams and new insights." Max looked up, his eye brows arched, his eyes searching mine to insure he had my full attention.

"What if," he began, "just what if our cancers did not arrive to harm us, to kill us, but were actually messengers to inform us of something we desperately needed to know about ourselves, something that we were doing or thinking that was harmful, probably even killing us?"

"What?" I was barely able to get out. "Where in the world did that idea come from?" My mind was swimming. I took a swig of coffee; I needed a jolt from the delicious brew to see if it would help me obtain some clarity.

Max waited. He was always good like that, always giving me time to let his ideas sink in. Then he added, "Remember, we're all carrying around cancer cells all the time. Why does the cancer suddenly decide to grow uncontrolled in some people?"

All I could do was stare at Max.

"And remember that the cancer cells are risking their own lives wildly growing in a body because if the body dies, they too will die.

"So, what if the cancer is really our friend, I mean aren't those cells a part of our bodies too, a part of who we are? What if their sole purpose in the growth spurt is not to kill us, but to try to communicate to us something we need to know, something maybe our soul, or whatever you call it is trying to tell us?"

Shaking my head in wonder, I was finally able to glimpse what Max was saying. This was big and I knew it.

"Why, this would revolutionize the way we treat cancer."

"You're damn right it would," he exclaimed, now aware that I was into the idea. "Not to belittle all the work the researchers have done trying to find a cure for cancer, but let's be honest here, cancer is still fully present in our world."

"Max, this is intriguing. I don't know if it's even accurate, but it certainly does resonate within me."

"Look at how we try to cure cancer now," he said, "Hell, we poison our system with chemotherapy and radiation treatments. There's something just not kosher about doing this."

"But how could we ever hear—or discover—what the cancer is trying to tell us?" I asked.

"My dream said this would be done by meditating, where we literally leave the physical world and enter into another dimension of reality. The dream revealed that it's during meditation where the communication process could take place." Max smiled.

"Furthermore," he said, "here's something even more far out. What if the cancers themselves discovered that once they had communicated the message and weren't able to shrink back to their former sizes, they then agreed to allow us to remove them as long as we agreed to place them in a container which would allow them to continuing living away from the host body?"

Wow! Where Max's original idea initially threw me, this one was now taking me even further into *never never land*.

"What if," Max was getting so excited I could tell he was about to jump out of his skin, "these containers of cancer, all over the world, were so appreciative of us maintaining their life forms that they began communicating to us another gift for keeping them alive? What if they began providing us with new cures for other diseases?"

I stared into Max's eyes for the longest time, enraptured over these incredibly provocative ideas until Max broke the reverie, sat back, took a deep drink of his coffee and said the most disarming thing, "Isn't this the best coffee you've ever tasted?"

The Art Of Living Does Not Mean We Should Try To Eliminate Our Troubles, But Instead Learn To Grow From Them.

—Maxwell Winston Stone

When A Bone
Breaks And Heals,
It Becomes Stronger
At The
Broken Place.

—Proverb

VICTOR FRANKL WAS A Jewish psychiatrist who headed the Department of Psychiatry in Vienna, Austria, the same position Sigmund Freud had held. However, during World War II, he was a prisoner in one of the worst Nazi concentration camps. One day they came and took his cap, shirt, belt, and shoes. The next day they took his trousers and underclothing, so he was completely naked. Then, they began to laugh at him; and they tried to humiliate him, but throughout it all he was able to maintain his composure.

After a few days, one of the Nazi guards who had been observing Frankl and was impressed with his inner strength, finally asked him how he was able to cope under such terrible abuse. Frankl responded, "You can rob me of everything I have. You can even take my wedding ring and throw it in the furnace to be melted down. But there is one thing you can never take from me—the last of the human freedoms, t*he freedom to choose my own attitude* in any given set of circumstances, the freedom to choose my own way!"

Frankl took this learning into his profession of psychiatry which greatly benefited many of his patients. Only by going through the horrors of the concentration camps was he able to learn such priceless knowledge. That, my friends, is what drives this point home.

To Face Every Adversity
As An Opportunity
Is One Of Life's
Greatest Secrets.

—MAXWELL WINSTON STONE

ONE OF THE GREAT preachers of last century was Dr. Ralph Sockman. He and his wife suffered a great tragedy with the death of their son. At first, it devastated the entire family. Eventually though, Dr. Sockman recovered from his grief and arrived at this unusual perception. He said, "There are parts of a ship, which taken by themselves, would sink. But when the parts of the ship are put together, they float!"

Then he explained further. "So it is with the events of our lives. Some are good, some are bad, some are happy, some are sad. But when they're all put together in the vessel of a human life, somehow they float.

"And we must never let any one, or two, or three events keep us from seeing the beauty of the larger whole."

Inside Each Person Is
Something Totally
Precious That No One
Else Possesses.

—MAXWELL WINSTON STONE

AS A KID GROWING UP, did you ever happen upon a scene where a butterfly was trying to emerge from a cocoon?

If you were lucky enough to observe this fascinating event, your first thoughts might have been what difficulty and pain the poor butterfly had to go through in order to forcefully squeeze itself out of the tightly compressing cocoon.

Most anyone watching this struggle would surely have great empathy as they watched the former caterpillar wiggle, squirm and force the now delicate butterfly out. Some might even wish to help the butterfly by cutting open the cocoon to help ease the butterfly's laborious feat. However, helping the butterfly to emerge in an easier manner would actually cause the butterfly to die.

Why? You see, the butterfly needs the struggle

because it is the struggle which squeezes out the moisture in the butterfly's wings, helps it to dry and thus, allows it the gift of being able to fly. Without this struggle, without all the squeezing and wiggling, the butterfly would emerge with its wings still full of moisture and, unable to fly, it would be an easy meal for any passing frog or toad.

Isn't this the same with us? If our life is too easy, if we didn't have to go through the struggles and pains life presents us, we also will find ourselves unable to fly, and therefore never able to achieve our innate potential.

Smooth seas do not make skillful sailors.

—AFRICAN PROVERB

The Troubles You Experience In Life Are There For A Reason—There Is Something You Need To Learn.

—MAXWELL WINSTON STONE

IN BANGKOK, THAILAND, a 10-foot tall, 5½ ton concrete Buddha stood in the courtyard just before the temple. It was the prized possession of the city.

One day, the people thought it would be more appropriate to have the Buddha moved into the temple. Gathering the strongest men with the best ropes and pulleys, they tried their best to move it, only to have it tip over and crash to the ground. At this same exact time, a monsoon rain came, leaving the villagers no other option than to wait until the rains stopped to finish their job.

The next morning, with the sun shining brightly, all the people gathered around their most prized possession only to see that it had been cracked in the fall. They began to cry and wail, until one of the priests who had been inspecting the crack saw something glimmering inside. With a pick, he began chipping away the cement until he soon exposed the world's largest chunk of gold—a 5½ ton, solid-gold Buddha.

History later disclosed that the Buddha had been originally created by the King of Siam around 1295. When war broke out, the people didn't want the Burmese army to get the gold so they covered it in cement. Thinking they would remove it later, they never had the opportunity as everyone with knowledge of it was killed in the battle.

This solid-gold, 5½ ton Buddha covered in cement stayed hidden for more than a hundred years.

It took a crisis—an adversity—for its hidden wealth and beauty to be exposed.

Seeing The Good In Everything Can Cost You—It Can Cost You Your Bitterness, Anger And Jealousy.

—Maxwell Winston Stone

...for my power is made perfect in weakness.

—II Corinthians 12:9

THE TRUTH ABOUT ADVERSITY bringing us gifts is easily seen in the action of an oyster, for the most extraordinary thing about an oyster is how it handles the adversity of irritations that enter into its shell quite uninvited.

Oysters are bivalves which mean that its shell is made up of two parts, or two valves. It also has an organ called a *mantle* which produces the oyster's shell from the minerals the oyster consumes as food. The material this mantel creates is called *nacre*.

This brief description is necessary in order to understand how a pearl is made. When an irritation or foreign substance enters into an oyster's life and slips between the mantle and the shell, it irritates the mantel. This in turn involuntarily causes the oyster to react by covering up the irritant with layers of the nacre substance, the same substance used to make its shell. This layering continues until a pearl is formed. So, a pearl is simply some kind of foreign substance covered with layers of nacre. It is also one of the most beautiful pieces of jewelry found on our planet.

We humans could learn from these mollusks how to handle the irritations that enter into our lives. How? By learning and then remembering each time that every adversity or irritant that enters into our lives will also bring with it a beautiful *pearl*.

Believe It Or Not, Most People Would Rather Die Than Change.

—MAXWELL WINSTON STONE

DO YOU KNOW HOW A lobster is able to grow bigger when its shell is so hard? It must shed its shell entirely. When its body begins feeling cramped inside its shell, it instinctively looks for a safe place to hide while the shell comes off. Then the pink membrane just inside it begins forming the basis of the next shell.

What is so frightening for the lobster is its vulnerability during this shedding process. It could be eaten by other fish or thrown into the rough coral reef. You see, the lobster must risk its life in order to grow.

This is the adversity the lobster *must* go through and it teaches us a valuable lesson: The only way to respond to life is to also grow and change, regardless of the risks involved. For without this, our lives will feel stifled, boring and unproductive. But with it, we can prepare ourselves for excitement and new adventures.

Whenever you fear adversity, remember the lobster, for we too must go through change and take risks in order to learn and grow.

 WOMAN FRIEND ONCE shared her devastation upon her husband's death. At first, she literally did not know how she was going to get through it.

But after time and much struggle, heartache, and forced change-of-lifestyle, she confessed to not only surviving, but actually growing in ways she never imagined. Forced now to find a job to support herself and two children she was shocked to discover that not all women had been as sheltered as she. Eyes wide open now, she began to better understand the difficulties working people went through, and therefore became more tolerant of others—more understanding of other people's lives and mistakes.

She humbly stated she had become a better human being. And only because of the adversity had her life become fuller and richer.

Thanks for the story, Wanda.

If You Are Still Alive,
It Is Never Too Late To
Be Whatever It Is That
You Want To Be.

—Maxwell Winston Stone

MAX TOLD ME A FABLE which beautifully discloses the uniqueness of the adversities that are in each of our lives. Here is the challenging fable.

"I heard a loud proclamation extended to all the world that each and every person was to bring all their griefs, burdens, and adversities, and throw them together in a heap. All of humankind lined up, the line extending far, far into the horizon where the earth and sky merged together. Some people had physical burdens, such as cancer, crippled limbs, blindness, heart conditions, obesity. Others brought adversities of loneliness, temptations, anxiety, depression, disappointment, lost ambition, and guilt. As each person laid down their burdens, whether real or imagined, the pile grew so high it reached the heavens.

"Then just as the last person relieved himself of

what he had been carrying, another loud proclamation was issued: Each person could now exchange their affliction for anyone else's. Eagerly each mortal selected a new burden, thinking they would now be better off.

"But strangely that was not the case, for now instead of joy, the whole earth became filled with moaning and wailing. People discovered very quickly their new condition was much worse than their former one.

"Taking pity on all humankind, an angel descended from Heaven and allowed each person to reclaim his or her original adversities or burdens.

"Upon awakening, the dream's message became vividly clear: *What if each person has their own specific burdens, and these burdens are the ones best suited for them, and them alone. What if ..."*

Remember That Many Fruits Do Not Turn Sweet Until The Cold Frost Settles Upon Them, Many Delicious Nuts Never Fall From The Tree Until The Frost Has Ripened And Opened Them. It Is The Same With Human Lives—They Never Become Sweet And Truly Beautiful Until Sorrow Has Been Experienced.

—Author Unknown

IN IRELAND, FOLLOWING THE potato famine when economic struggles were the norm of the day, one large Irish family decided they had to get to America to find a better way of life. The father began working three jobs, when he could get them, the four boys worked wherever they could find odd jobs while the three girls and the mother sold butter and eggs, and did laundry and housekeeping jobs for the richer families. All the money the family accumulated went towards one goal; paying the cost of tickets for a boat ride that would transport them all to the opportunity-filled United States.

After much hard work, the family finally earned enough money. At the ticket office, the proud father discovered he could only afford to purchase *non-refundable* tickets for his family. Since they were certain nothing could stop them from going, he gladly paid. Plans were made to leave their home and take a ship leaving in only two weeks time.

Then the unexpected happened. One of the sons was bitten by a rabid dog. Initially thinking this would prove to be no hindrance to their cherished trip, everything changed when the local veterinarian informed him the lad was required by law to be quarantined for four weeks. The family was crushed. All their dreams and hopes of going to America were now utterly destroyed. Remember, the tickets had been non-refundable.

The father became quite bitter at God for the misfortune He had bestowed on them, began drinking up all their money and cursed God incessantly.

One day upon entering his favorite pub, he overheard some men discussing the news that a boat to America had hit an iceberg and sunk causing the deaths of fifteen hundred and two people. Shocked, the father asked the name of the ship. When he heard the name, the **TITANIC**, his face went pale for that was the very ship they were to have sailed on.

Putting down his drink, the thankful father hurried home to tell his family of the news. Gathering his family all together, the humbled man had his family get down on their knees and give thanks to God for saving all of their lives. What had looked like the worst thing ... was the very thing that had saved their lives.

Prosperity Teaches
Us Little;
Adversity Much.

—Maxwell Winston Stone

THERE'S A STORY FROM long ago, where the people of a small village were upset over having poor crop harvests.

So they prayed to God for a promise that their crops would have only rain and sunshine, and never the harsh north wind. As the story goes, God granted their explicit wish to have only sun and rain, and no harsh winds.

The villagers were excited to see how tall their corn grew and how thick became their wheat. However, when the time came to reap the crops, their joy turned into horror. Turning to God, they proclaimed, "You have not fulfilled your promise Lord. Why?"

God responded, "Oh but I did my children. I gave you exactly what you asked for."

The villagers cried, "But why does our corn stock not have corn, our wheat stock not have wheat?"

"Because," God explained, "you did not have the harsh north wind. And without it, there can be no pollination, and therefore no crops."

The Soul Would
Have No Rainbow
Had The Eyes
No Tears.

—JOHN VANCE CHENEY (1848-1922)
AMERICAN POET, ESSAYIST, AND LIBRARIAN

I asked God for strength,
   that I might achieve,
I was made weak, that I might
   learn humbly to obey.
I asked for health, that I might
   do greater things,
I was given infirmity, that I might
   do better things.
I asked for riches, that I might
   be happy,
I was given poverty, that I might
   be wise.
I asked for power, that I might
   have the praise of men,

I was given weakness, that I might
feel the need of God.
I asked for all things, that I might
enjoy life,
I was given life, that I might
enjoy all things.
I got nothing that I asked for—
but everything I had hoped for.
Almost despite myself, my
unspoken prayers were answered.
I am among all men,
most richly blessed.

—Anonymous

"This is one of my favorite poems."
—Max

Adversity Introduces
A Person
To Themselves.

—Epictetus (AD 55-AD 135)
Roman Sage and Philosopher

IF YOU EVER

If you ever need to know, you will.
If you ever feel, don't flee.

If you ever hurt, release it.
If you ever fly, soar.

If you ever cry, embrace it.
If you ever smile, pass it on.
If you ever die, know you have lived.

If you ever sin, don't sweat it.
If you ever love, give up hate.
If you ever hate, it's a slow death.

If you ever hug, repeat often.
If you ever make love, keep it up.

If you ever take walks, try skipping.
If you ever receive, give back.

If you are ever served, tip heavily.
If you ever forgive, you win.

If you ever feel poor, donate yourself.
If you ever feel rich, give even more.

If you ever stumble,
know you are not alone.
If you ever have a true friend,
know its rarity.

If you ever considered trying,
you might.
If you ever thought you could, you can.

If you ever believe you can,
it's already done.

Eat lots. Laugh Often. Live Fully.

—Ernie Carwile

Perhaps All The Dragons
In Our Lives Are
Princes Or Princesses
Who Are Only Waiting
To See Us Once
Beautiful And Brave.

—Rainer Mariea Rilke (1887-1926)
Bohemian—Austrian Poet

Barn's Burnt Down,
Now I Can See
The Moon.

—Mizuta Masahide (1657-1723)
17th Century Japanese Poet and Samurai

REMEMBER THAT THE Stratavarious violin, perhaps the greatest violin ever created, was harvested from only the toughest forest in Northern Croatia. This maple wood, known for its extreme density, resulted in slow growth brought about by the harshest winds and weather conditions in the frigid Croatians winters.

Why did the violin maker use such wood? ... Because only the toughest wood, the wood that had been grown under the most adverse circumstances, could produce the *sweetest* sounds in the entire world?

Could this be the same for you and me?

There Is A Light
Behind Every
Shadow.

—Maxwell Winston Stone

HE AWOKE EARLIER THAN usual, just as the first morning light secretly crept into their bedroom illuminating what had once been only dark shadows. Turning his head slightly to the right, he watched as his wife's face became visible, distinct.

Surprisingly, visions suddenly appeared of when they had first started dating. She had knocked his socks off the first time he saw her; her cuteness, the light freckles which speckled across her tiny nose and cheeks, the glow that always seemed to emanate from her whenever he was around, and her fabulous body; just slightly overweight, she had reminded him of a ripe Georgia peach just waiting to be plucked. Pleasant feelings flooded his body.

Then, just as fast as they appeared, the visions receded, returning him to the present; reality. He now remembered that her once slightly overweight body had ballooned up, broadening her face, hips, waist and legs. Now her breasts sagged.

Of course, he honestly acknowledged, his body had also changed and not for the better. He was no longer the thin, young man he had once been. Sighing deeply, he closed his eyes hoping for a life do-over, all the while the uncomfortable questions kept turning in his head like an old, broken record. Where had his life gone? What had happened to the once *hot* relationship they had shared, the excitement, the wild sex, and the love? Where had it all gone?

His job wasn't any better. Hell, it was a drag, too. Somehow he had just never lived up to his potential, had never been able to climb the long corporate ladder, never achieved much at all, phrases his wife often pointed out.

His thoughts turned to his children. There never seemed to be enough time for them. There was always something else to do—work, the yard, repairs to the house, fixing the car. His oldest was fourteen; the youngest twelve. He sadly realized he had not only missed out on their early years, he was *still* missing out on what was happening in their lives now. What were their dreams, their aspirations? What subjects did they enjoy the most at school? Who were their best friends?

Flinching as the pain jolted through his head, he remembered his doctor's appointment later in the day. These sharp painful sessions had concerned both he and his wife. He tried to laugh it off, calling it a "roving cancer," an expression they had adopted whenever an unusual pain was felt in their aging bodies. But then the pain persisted, increased in both intensity and frequency, and didn't go away; thus, today's doctor's appointment.

* * * * * *

Later that same day, the doctor ushered him into his office looking grim, frightening him more than his own earlier fears; then the words, "You have inoperable brain cancer."

Numb. Of course he felt numb; I mean how is one supposed to feel hearing you're going to die? But it was like he was somehow outside his body when he heard the doctor's dire prognostication. Initially he thought it couldn't be meant for him; it had to be for someone else. He finally mumbled, "How long?" and heard the sentence of "only one to two years."

There was no memory of driving home; only

when the garage door opened was he jolted aware.

Entering the family room, as usual neither his two children nor wife even acknowledged him. Dropping down into his old chair, no one still seemed aware of him. Only when he quietly stated, "I have inoperable brain cancer," did everyone freeze, only then did his wife speak. "What did you say?

Repeating what the doctor had told him, suddenly everyone moved at exactly the same time; rushed over to him. Condolences were expressed, care, and concern, words he had not heard from anyone in his family for what seemed an eternity. In only a second his life was transformed.

It was like time had moved backwards to when the family had been close, loving. His children volunteered to help in any way possible; his wife too. In the drop of a hat, he regained the family he had always dreamt about; once had.

Even his boss responded with compassion, telling him to take some time off, reminding him they had the best health care insurance money could buy.

In the days to come everything miraculously became new, even though he didn't feel well all the time; the relationship with his children, he and his wife's sex life returned again to a loving and passionate one, and his job took on new meaning.

(RUSH FORWARD To Just Under Three Years)

The same man is in the hospital bed near death. He had requested a temporary reduction in the pain medications so he could think, reflect back on his life, especially the past three years.

He recalled how lousy his life had been going until the news of his brain cancer.

He also remembered how everything had suddenly changed; the love his family began sharing, the new respect bestowed upon him by his boss as the quality of his work soared.

He was confused. At first he attributed it to the drugs that still remained in his body, but the new insight persisted; that with the onset of cancer his life had become richer, infinitely better than before.

Suddenly, the most daunting, haunting question of all clearly appeared: Was the cancer actually a gift in disguise? Was the greatest adversity that came into his life … was it actually the one greatest gift?

Epilogue

CERTAINLY I HAD BEEN vaguely aware of the concept that every adversity brings with it a gift, though I had never truly believed nor incorporated it into my practical consciousness.

However, after doing research for this book, after reading so many quotes and stories advocating this little maxim, something began shifting within me. I began to review my life in a totally different way. I developed a whole new paradigm for viewing my past adversities, and then somehow ... some way ... everything changed. My thinking was drastically altered and it was as if I had been reborn.

This is what Max and I are encouraging for you—to really grasp this truth that every adversity which enters into your life brings with it a gift especially designed for you; actually custom-tailored for your own specific life. Or as Albert Einstein supposedly said in his later life, "I have come to believe there is a plan after all!"

About the Author

ERNIE CARWILE was born in Munich, Germany and has lived throughout the world. He is a graduate of the University of Missouri and the Iliff School of Theology in Denver, Colorado.

After high school he sold cemetery plots door-to-door in Hannibal, Missouri, and while attending college, he drove one of the huge trucks for Peabody Coal Mine. Mr. Carwile has been an Air force Officer, heavyweight boxer and a Methodist and Congregational minister.

As a celebrated author and master storyteller, Carwile has been featured extensively in the national media including *Good Morning America, Inside Edition, CNN, Associated Press, Court TV, Clear Channel Radio, the Los Angeles Times and the Rocky Mountain News.*

His books have received a great review from the most prestigious *Library Journal*, as well as Endorsements/Thank You's from the President of the United States, twelve U.S. Governors and such prominent collegiate football coaches as Steve Spurrier. They also have been translated into five foreign languages.

www.ingramcontent.com/pod-product-compliance
Lightning Source LLC
Chambersburg PA
CBHW060817050426
42449CB00008B/1698